Fire and Forgiveness

Young Palmetto Books

Kim Shealy Jeffcoat,
Series Editor

FIRE AND FORGIVENESS

A Nun's Truce with General Sherman

MARTHA DUNSKY

Illustrated by
MONICA WYRICK

THE UNIVERSITY OF
SOUTH CAROLINA PRESS

© 2019 Martha Dunsky Caprarotta

Published by the University of South Carolina Press
Columbia, South Carolina 29208

www.sc.edu/uscpress

Manufactured in the United States of America

28 27 26 25 24 23 22 21 20 19
10 9 8 7 6 5 4 3 2

Library of Congress Cataloging-in-Publication Data
can be found at http://catalog.loc.gov/.

ISBN: 978-1-61117-985-9 (hardcover)
ISBN: 978-1-61117-986-6 (ebook)

Dedicated to all peacemakers.

ACKNOWLEDGMENTS

Heartfelt thanks to my sister Monica Wyrick, who's responsible for this book's existence. When she learned the dramatic history of Mother Baptista's letter to General Sherman and what befell students at the Ursuline Convent School during Columbia's burning, she envisioned a children's book. I am fortunate that she asked me to write it, and that she agreed to illustrate it. Her vivid drawings bring the characters and story to life. Moreover, Monica has been a true collaborator through every step of the creative process, from providing constructive feedback on my early and revised drafts, to tracking down Mother Baptista's headstone.

My deep gratitude to Jonathan Haupt, former director at the University of South Carolina Press and sponsoring editor for my manuscript. As a first-time author, I greatly appreciated his guidance, belief in my book, and patience in answering my many questions.

Thanks also to John Sherrer, director of Cultural Resources at Historic Columbia, who graciously read my manuscript for historical accuracy, and provided a sketch of the Hampton-Preston House and insight into the people who were enslaved there; Jake Wyrick for his feedback on my first draft and his legal counsel on my contract; and Sister Bridget Nolan, archivist for the Ursuline Sisters of Youngstown, Ohio, for her expertise on the habits nuns wore in the past.

INTRODUCTION

In 1861 war broke out in the United States between the Northern and Southern states. They disagreed on how much power the central government held over the states, especially on slavery. The North wanted to forbid slavery in new states forming in the west. The South feared that would lead to outlawing slavery in all states. The end of slavery would financially ruin Southern states. They depended greatly on slave labor on plantations, and in cities. In 1860, almost half of the people living in Columbia, South Carolina were enslaved.

The South believed states had the right to separate (or "secede") from the United States. In December 1860, South Carolina was the first state to secede. A total of eleven Southern states seceded and formed the Confederate States of America. In April 1861 the Confederate states and the Northern (or "Union") states began fighting the Civil War.

Almost four years later, a weak Confederate army was retreating as General William T. Sherman led the Union army through the South. When Sherman entered Columbia, South Carolina, he promised the mother superior of an Ursuline Convent that her nuns and students would be safe. But that promise was not kept. The convent and much of Columbia were destroyed by fire.

This story is based on eyewitness accounts of what happened that night and how the nun and General Sherman made their own peace. Jane, Clara and Sister Beatrice are fictional characters. But the lessons they teach about forgiveness and peacemaking are real.

Booming Cannons

Thursday Dawn, February 16, 1865

Jane woke abruptly. The bedroom she shared with three other girls was dark and silent. Sister Beatrice hadn't knocked on the door to get them up for mass. Then Jane heard it—a booming sound from far away. Cannons! The terrible war had come to Columbia!

General Sherman had marched his Union army north after capturing Savannah, while the Confederate armies had retreated. Now Sherman's army was across the Congaree River, just outside Columbia. Confederate soldiers in Columbia were firing at the enemy across the water.

Most people had already fled the city. They feared the Union army would seek revenge on Columbia for leading South Carolina to be the first state to secede. But 200 students ages five to eighteen remained at the Ursuline Convent School for Girls. The Mother Superior, Sister Baptista Lynch, decided weeks ago it was the safest place for them. Now as cannon fire sent a chill down Jane's spine, she prayed Mother Baptista was right.

Silently, Jane slipped out of bed to peek out the window. As her feet slid into her slippers, she felt something gooey. Startled,

Jane pulled off one slipper and smelled the sticky stuff. Molasses! How did it get there? Who would do such a thing? Jane could think of only one person—Clara!

Clara was a new student who didn't like Jane from the start. When Jane beat Clara in the spelling bee, Clara started calling her "Jane the Giraffe." Jane was indeed a head taller than her fellow nine-year-olds, and even some of the older girls.

Jane took after her father, who towered above six feet. Before he left for war, he made Jane promise to always stand tall and be brave. So, Jane was proud of her height. Still, she got even with Clara by calling her "Freckle Face," for Clara had more freckles than the night sky had stars.

Now the name-calling had grown into a mean act! Well, Jane would give Clara a taste of her own medicine. Carefully, Jane dug the molasses from her slippers and her toes. She crept silently to the wash stand and pushed the sticky stuff into Clara's hairbrush. The cannons rumbled again. *This was war!*

MIGHTY FORTRESS

Thursday Morning, February 16, 1865

The girls marched orderly behind the nuns down Main Street on their way to mass. The distant cannon fire quickened the pace of people still fleeing the city. Jane and her classmates shivered nervously until they reached St. Peter's Catholic Church. It stood solid and strong, with pointed spires that reminded Jane of a castle. Surely no harm would come to them in this mighty fortress of God!

During mass Clara sang a solo. Her face blushed as red as her hair, which stuck out in clumps around her face. There hadn't been time to wash the molasses from her hair. Some of the girls snickered, and Jane smiled to herself. But, despite her humiliation, Clara's voice was strong and clear. "Faith of our fathers, living still! In spite of dungeon, fire, and sword . . ."

The snickering stopped as the girls heard Clara's angelic singing. A nearby statue of Jesus with open arms seemed to offer Clara safety from dungeon, fire, and—unkind classmates, thought Jane guiltily. She glanced away in shame and found Sister Beatrice giving her a knowing look.

Friend of the General

Thursday Afternoon, February 16, 1865

Classes ended early that day. No one could study with the loud cannon blasts outside. It was more frightening now that the Union forces were firing on Columbia. Shells hit the new State House just six blocks from the convent. Many girls hid under their beds with pillows over their ears. Jane longed to join them, but Sister Beatrice sent her to the Mother Superior's office.

Mother Baptista was an imposing figure with a regal air. Her piercing gray eyes tolerated no nonsense. Under that gaze, Jane quickly admitted her crime. "But it wasn't my fault! Clara started it!"

The nun shook her head. "It doesn't matter who *starts* a war. What matters is that someone *ends* it. The longer it lasts, the harder it is to make peace. I want you to end it *today.*"

"How can I do that?" Jane asked. "Clara hates me! And I don't know why."

Mother Baptista sighed. "Clara is a new student with few friends, while you have many." She paused, and then added quietly, "Clara has been upset since her father was taken prisoner of war. Did you know that?" Jane shook her head in dumb surprise. If her own father was ever taken prisoner or hurt, she would be devastated!

Mother Baptista took Jane's hand. "Clara needs you as a *friend,* not an enemy. I know it's not easy asking for forgiveness. Are you brave enough to do it?" Jane remembered her promise to her father and nodded in agreement.

"Good!" the nun grinned. "Apologize to Clara. And give her a compliment. Tell her something you like about her, to start your friendship." Jane opened her mouth to object, but the nun stopped her. "God made us all. There is *good* in everyone, if you look for it."

Just then, Father O'Connell burst into the room. "There won't be a battle! General Beauregard fears the Union army would destroy our city. Beauregard and his soldiers will leave Columbia tonight, and General Hampton's cavalry will leave in the morning."

"No battle? Thank the Lord!" Mother Baptista breathed.

"Yes, *but,*" the priest said gravely, "our mayor will surrender our city in the morning to General Sherman. Mother Baptista, you knew Sherman when you taught his daughter in Ohio. Is he as fierce and evil as they say?"

"There is good in everyone," Jane spoke up, surprising the priest who hadn't seen her. "Mother Baptista, won't General Sherman protect us, if he's your friend?"

The nun smiled at Jane, and said, "You are right. I will write my friend General Sherman a letter and ask for his protection."

THE LETTER AND A PROMISE

Friday Morning and Afternoon, February 17, 1865

Early the next morning the Confederate cavalry left Columbia, and the mayor surrendered the city to General Sherman. Soon after, Jane joined other girls at the convent's windows to see the Union soldiers marching down Main Street! They were quite a sight with shining swords and gleaming guns. Their bright banners whipped about in the strong winds of that day. Endless rows of soldiers marched by on foot, followed by the cavalry on horses. Finally, the terrifying cannons the girls had heard yesterday rumbled by.

Many citizens jeered at the passing army. Some wished the Confederate armies had fought to defend Columbia. But Jane was relieved no more cannons or guns would be fired, and no one hurt. She prayed every night for the war to end so that no one else would be wounded or killed, especially her father.

Father O'Connell returned from General Sherman's headquarters with a Union soldier to guard the convent. Later that morning, the girls saw a big blaze in the distance as Union soldiers burned the railroad depot. "Don't worry," the priest reassured the girls. "Sherman says we'll be safe in our convent. We are not a threat."

Nonetheless, Mother Baptista wrote her letter to General Sherman. She had been a good teacher to his daughter and was a friend of Sherman's wife, who was a devout Catholic. The nun asked for protection for her convent and her students and nuns. Sherman answered her letter with a note, promising the convent and everyone in it would be safe from harm.

Mother Baptista was pleased with Sherman's reply. She wasn't pleased, however, when Jane reported she hadn't made peace with Clara. "I did apologize," Jane said, frowning. "And I told her she sings beautifully. But she stuck out her tongue and ran away!"

"Most wars aren't ended overnight," the nun admitted. "You must try again. Give her a second chance." When Jane looked doubtful, Mother Baptista reminded her, "Jesus said, 'Blessed are the *peacemakers,* for they will be called *children* of God.'"

"Yes," Jane nodded. "But why must children be peacemakers? Adults can't end a war that has gone on for years."

Mother Baptista looked at Jane with tears in her eyes. "True, it's not easy for adults to forgive and make peace. That's why it is so important for you and Clara to learn how. If we want to have any peace in this world, it must begin with the *children.*"

Preparing to Flee

Friday Evening, February 17, 1865

Despite Sherman's promise, the nuns prepared the girls in case they had to flee the convent. They were told how to line up and how to behave. The smaller girls would walk between the bigger students. Each girl was to dress warmly and make a small bundle of extra clothing, for the winter winds were strong that day.

As Jane prepared her bundle in the bedroom next to Clara, she remembered her promise to Mother Baptista. "Clara," Jane said hesitantly. "I hope Sister Beatrice is right about the war ending soon. Then your father can come home. And mine, too."

Before Clara could reply, Sister Beatrice entered the room. "Jane, the taller girls will carry a torch, and walk at the ends of each row. Can you do this?"

Jane agreed, though she knew it would be safer to walk in the middle. Then she looked at her bundle. How would she carry it and the torch?

As if reading Jane's thoughts, Clara spoke. "I'll carry your bundle. I can manage both yours and mine."

"Oh! Thank you!" Jane said in surprise. Clara gave her a slight nod before turning away.

When darkness fell, the girls could see fires pop up

throughout the city. When the evening Angelus bells rang, many of the girls joined the nuns in the convent chapel to pray. Jane prayed for courage to carry the torch bravely if they had to leave.

A short time later, they heard shouts from angry men breaking in the chapel door. The men wanted to steal the gold chalice and silver candlesticks, not knowing the priest had removed them to a safer place.

"Girls, it is time to leave," Mother Baptista said in a loud, calm voice. Her cool demeanor steadied the girls as they quickly lined up in the long main hall.

The intruders' cries grew angrier when they didn't find the gold or silver. Any minute they would break into the rest of the convent.

Jane's hands gripped her torch like a vise and held it high. Eager to be gone, the girls marched briskly into the cold night.

Walking Through Fire

Friday Night, February 17, 1865

Outside, Jane blinked in surprise. So many buildings and houses were on fire that the streets were bright from the blazes. Father O'Connell led their procession, holding a crucifix up high for all to see. The nuns followed him in their flowing black habits. The girls marched behind in neat ranks like a miniature army.

Noise and chaos were everywhere. Women, children, and elderly men ran out of some of the burning homes, screaming and crying. Thieves ran about, carrying their loot from empty houses and shops. Angry men and soldiers shouted and started new fires. Gusty winds spread flames from one building to another.

Jane's hands trembled in fear, and she almost dropped the torch. To calm herself, she imagined her father walking beside her, shielding her from danger. She glanced at the smaller girls beside her. Their faces were white and frightened, but no one whimpered or cried. Thieves and soldiers stopped and watched in silence as the courageous little troop filed by. No one came near or harmed them.

Fires roared on either side as the nuns and students marched down the middle of Main Street toward St. Peter's Church. Despite the cold night, Jane felt the heat of the flames. She thought of Moses and the Jewish people who walked through the raging Red Sea. But instead of walls of water, *they* were walking through walls of fire!

The three blocks felt more like three miles. Jane said a prayer of thanks to see the church standing unburned. Tonight, it truly was a safe fortress. As she entered the arched doorway, the priest pried the torch from her stiff fingers. Once inside, some of the girls broke down and cried. The nuns comforted them and urged them to lie down on the pews.

A few nuns had stayed behind at the convent to protect it from fire. They arrived at the church with terrible news. The convent was engulfed in flames. Their home, their school, and all their belongings were destroyed.

Jane lay down on a pew, stunned. She closed her eyes, but could not erase the awful images of the flames, the homeless families, the shouting men. Tears ran down her cheeks. As she felt her courage slip away, the comforting faces of Jesus and her father appeared. "Stay with me," she whispered, until sleep overcame her.

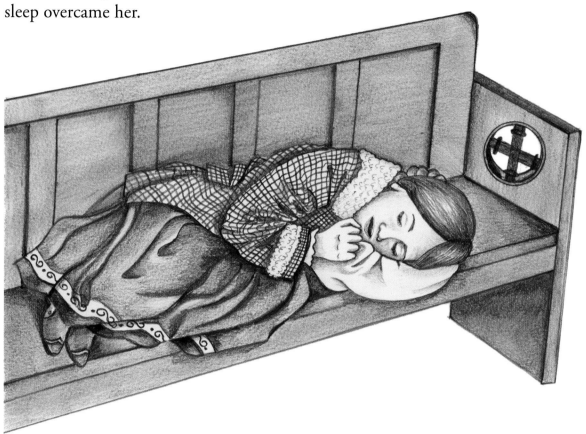

HIDING IN THE CEMETERY

Saturday, the Wee Hours of Morning, February 18, 1865

Their ordeal was far from over. The girls' brief sleep was broken by a group of angry soldiers shouting at everyone to leave the church! They were going to blow it up!

There was no time to think. The nuns, girls and Father O'Connell rushed out of the church in a panic. They flew through the churchyard and broke through bushes, into the nearby cemetery. With nowhere else to go, they hid behind the tombstones, catching their breath. Many of the girls began sobbing. What would happen next? Would ghosts arise from the graves and scare them away, as well?

Some Union officers nearby saw the group run from the church, and asked what was wrong. "Your soldiers are going to blow up our church!" Sister Beatrice declared.

"No, they won't!" the good officers protested. "We'll stop them!" True to their word, they ran off the unruly soldiers.

The nuns and girls were too frightened, however, to leave their hiding places in the cemetery. They huddled together for warmth, having left their bundles in the church. Jane opened her coat and invited a small shivering girl inside. Clara followed Jane's example, wrapping her coat around a younger girl.

As the girls watched from behind the tombstones, fires encircled the cemetery. The high winds roared, carrying smoke and ashes in the air. They burned Jane's eyes and throat. She covered her face with her hankie, but could not shut out the shouts and screams in the streets. The cemetery became crowded with families that were now homeless. All the while, Mother Baptista kept vigil like a mother hen, keeping her nuns and girls together and protected from strangers.

The small girls with Jane and Clara cried and called for their mothers. Clara began to sing softly. "Sleep holy babe, thine angels watch around . . ." Her soothing voice quieted the youngsters. Finally, they closed their eyes and nodded off. Jane envied their sleep. She thought the night and its horrors would never end.

Forgiveness and Friendship

Saturday Sunrise, February 18, 1865

A gentle shake awakened Jane. "Look!" Clara said. Surprised that she had dozed, Jane opened her eyes. The flames were gone, but she saw only thick smoke, rising all around the cemetery. "There!" Clara pointed upward.

Jane looked up. High above the smoke, the cross atop St. Peter's steeple shone in the faint sunrise. The church was not burned! The Union officers had saved it. Jane and Clara smiled at each other. "You were so brave last night," Clara said quietly. "I'm glad you were with me."

"You were brave too," Jane replied. "And your singing comforted the girls—and me."

This time, Clara didn't stick out her tongue. Instead, she said with a sob, "Oh, Jane! I'm sorry for everything I did that hurt you. Can we forgive each other, and start over?"

"Yes!" Jane gave her a long hug. "Oh, Clara, what a story we have to tell our fathers when they come home! Let's pray that happens soon." With that, they ended their war and started a great friendship.

A Truce in the Ashes

Saturday Morning, February 18, 1865

Later that morning, the nuns and girls gathered in the churchyard. They were grateful their church was saved, but the convent school and much of the city had burned to the ground. Where would they go now? Mother Baptista looked exhausted and pale. She had stayed awake all night, watching over them. Jane decided to cheer her up.

"Mother Baptista, Clara and I made up!" Jane said with a bright smile. "She carried my bundle when I held the torch. And she sang to stop the younger girls from crying. You were right about giving her a second chance."

The news brought a smile to the nun's worn face. Before she could answer, a Union officer approached. Mother Baptista stood up straight, her smile replaced by a stern look. Jane heard the nuns nearby whisper, "It's General Sherman!"

He was tall and lean with a narrow face, sharp nose, and a reddish beard and moustache. His dark blue uniform was covered in more brass buttons than Jane could count. Stars on his shoulders declared his importance. Yet the famous general looked nervous as he faced the nun.

"Good morning, Mother Superior," he said. Then he removed his cigar from his mouth and apologized for it. Clumsily, he tried to talk his way out of the trouble he was in. "I told my men to destroy only certain public buildings. *Not* homes or convents! But those winds blew the fires out of control," he explained. "And your citizens shouldn't have left so much liquor in the city. It caused some of my men to—uh—celebrate a bit too much."

His excuses only upset Mother Baptista more. Her eyes were full of fire, and she looked as daunting as any general as she spoke. "General Sherman, is this how you keep your promise to a nun? Our convent is destroyed. We have nothing, and nowhere to go."

At that, the general stopped making excuses. He said he was truly sorry, and he offered her any house left standing to replace her convent.

"I don't think the houses are yours to give," Mother Baptista began, then paused. Jane held her breath. Would the nun refuse Sherman's apology? Or would she give him a second chance, as she had asked Jane to do with Clara? Would these adults end their war? Or could only children be peacekeepers?

Mother Baptista glanced at Jane as if also recalling what she had told the girl. Then the nun continued in a calmer voice. "But, General, when I do find a suitable place for my nuns and students, I will thank you to move us and provide food." Sherman nodded, and Jane breathed in relief. The nun and the general had reached a temporary truce.

Keeping a Promise for Peace

Saturday Noon, February 18, 1865

The first person to help the convent's refugees was a Union officer's widow, who lived next door to the church. She brought hot coffee and bread to the cold and hungry girls and nuns. Jane whispered in surprise to Clara, "Her husband was killed fighting Confederate soldiers, but she is kind to us. Like the Union officers who saved our church."

"Yes," Clara agreed. "It gives me hope that my father is being treated fairly in prison."

At noon, General Sherman sent Colonel Ewing with ambulances to take the nuns and girls to the Methodist Female College. There they would find temporary housing. The colonel also gave them meat, sugar, coffee, tea, flour and hardtack.

After Mother Baptista thanked the colonel, Sister Beatrice and Jane brought her bad news. They overheard two soldiers talking about the Preston House. It had survived the fire because the Union army was using it as its headquarters. But they were going to burn it down when the army left Columbia in the morning.

"This cannot happen!" Mother Baptista exclaimed. The Preston family and General Hampton's grandfather, who previously owned the house, had been friends to the Ursuline nuns. Suddenly, Mother Baptista remembered Sherman's offer—she could have any house left standing. At first, she had dismissed that offer because no house in Columbia was large enough to replace the 70-room convent. But she might save one house to repay its owners for their past kindness to her nuns. She quickly wrote a note to Sherman, asking for the Preston House.

Jane ran the note to the colonel, telling him it was urgent for the general. Mother Baptista and Jane waited anxiously for an answer. The two soldiers had said they were eager to burn General Hampton's family home "to teach the Confederate general a lesson." Did General Sherman feel the same way? Would he refuse to hand over the house despite his promise?

Finally, Sherman's note arrived. Mother Baptista tore it open, and relief erased the worry on her face. "The Preston House will not be burned!" she read. "General Sherman has given it to us."

Jane clapped her hands in joy. Sherman had kept his second promise! Then Jane realized something more important than saving the house had happened. In the middle of a terrible war, two adults from opposite sides had made peace.

Having just experienced some horrors of war, Jane understood why Mother Baptist had insisted that Jane make peace with Clara. All forgiveness and peace-making was important—whether between two young girls, or a nun and a general, or two armies. Nothing mattered more than making peace. For only with peace could hope and life flourish in the world.

MAP KEY

Yellow indicates areas that were burned

 Site where Union cannons were fired

 Site where Confederate cannons were fired

 St. Peter's Church and Cemetery

 Ursuline Convent

 Hampton-Preston House

 Sherman's Headquarters

 South Carolina State House

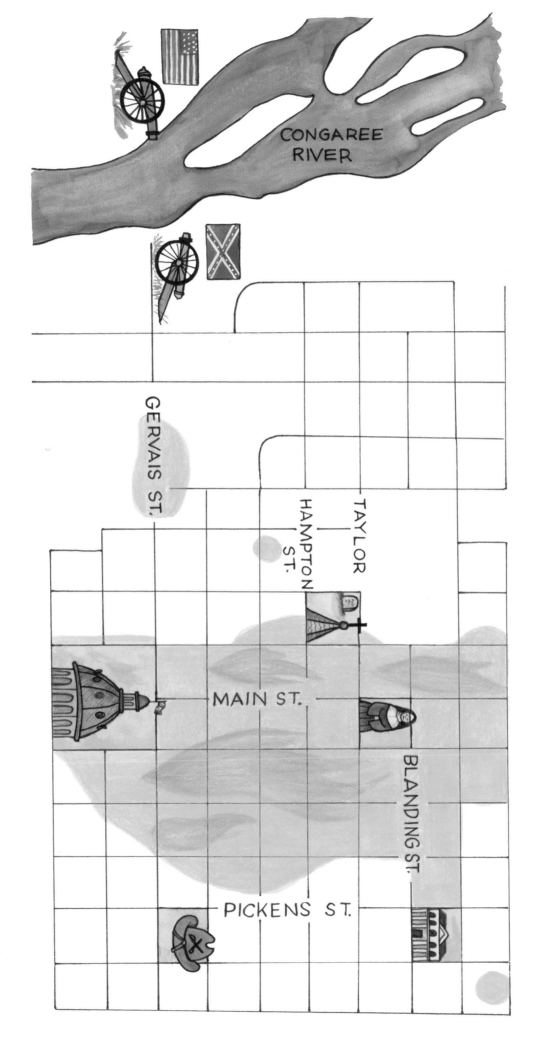

1865 Columbia map showing burned areas. Illustration by Monica Wyrick.

CONGAREE RIVER

GERVAIS ST.

TAYLOR

HAMPTON ST.

MAIN ST.

BLANDING ST.

PICKENS ST.

The Rest of the Story

Burning of Columbia

The fires of February 17, 1865, destroyed about one-third of Columbia. Political, military and transportation buildings were burned, as well as some commercial and private properties. Some say the fires were set by Union soldiers. Others blame the spreading fires on strong winds and bales of cotton that Confederate soldiers left in the streets. General Sherman denied ordering the burning, but he did order the destruction of anything of military value.

Ruins seen from the capitol, Columbia, S.C., 1865. Photographed by George N. Barnard. 165-SC-53. *National Archives Identifier:* 533426.

The End of War, with Peace Between Generals

William T. Sherman (between 1860 and 1870). Retrieved from the Library of Congress, https://www.loc.gov/item/cwp2003003503/PP/.

After leaving Columbia, General Sherman and his troops marched north through the Carolinas, destroying everything that could help the Confederate forces. Although criticized for his harsh policies, Sherman's strategy helped to end the Civil War. The Confederate armies of North and South Carolina, Georgia, and Florida surrendered in April 1865.

At the surrender, General Sherman gave the starving Confederate men ten days' food rations. The Confederate commander, General Joseph E. Johnston, never forgot that kind gesture. When Sherman died in 1891, Johnston was a pallbearer in the military funeral procession.

The End of Slavery

During the war, in 1863, President Lincoln wrote the Emancipation Proclamation. This declared all the enslaved in the South were now free (although Confederate states still considered them enslaved). About 179,000 formerly enslaved people and free black men fought for the Union army. Another 19,000 served in the Union navy. In April 1865, just before the war ended, the 13th Amendment to the Constitution was passed. It permanently outlawed slavery in the United States.

Hampton-Preston House

Hampton-Preston Mansion, February 17–19, 1865. Historic Columbia collection, HCF 2007.4.5

After General Sherman gave the Preston House to Mother Baptista, some of her nuns and pupils stayed there until the war ended a few months later. Then Mother Baptista returned the house to the Preston family.

Today known as the Hampton-Preston House, it is one of Columbia's oldest and most beloved historic homes. Built in 1818, the mansion was restored in the late 1960s and opened in 1970 to the public. Visitors can tour the gardens and house and learn about the enslaved men, women, and children who labored there.

Mother Baptista Lynch

Mother Baptista Lynch helped establish the Ursuline Convent in Columbia in 1858. Her cool bravery during the burning of Columbia and her swift actions to save the Hampton-Preston House make her a beloved figure in Columbia's history.

After the war, Mother Baptista and her nuns moved several times before a new convent was built. She died in 1887 at the age of 65, having served 37 years in religious life. She is buried in St. Peter's Cemetery, where she once watched over her convent's students as Columbia burned. Her headstone reads, "May Light and Peace and Rest Eternal be her portion in the Bosom of God."

Mother Baptista Lynch's headstone.
Photographed by the author.

Ursuline Convent School for Girls

Catholic Convent, Columbia, S.C., 1865. Carte-de-visite by Richard Wearn (Photographs Wearn 4).
Courtesy of the South Caroliniana Library, University of South Carolina, Columbia, S.C.

In 1865 the Ursuline Convent School for Girls on Blanding Street housed 200 students. The nuns taught English, foreign languages, singing, art, embroidery, and music (piano, harp, and guitar). On February 17, 1865, fire destroyed the convent when Columbia was burned.

After using several temporary locations, the nuns built a new Ursuline Convent in 1891 on Assembly Street. Years later this was torn down to make way for the present St. Peter's Catholic School, which opened in 1992.

St. Peter's Catholic Church and Cemetery

St. Peter's Catholic Church was first built in 1824. It survived the burning of Columbia and was used for another forty years. In the early 1900s, a new church was built on the site.

Behind St. Peter's Church is the cemetery where the Ursuline Convent School nuns and students hid during the burning of Columbia. Mother Baptista Lynch is buried there.

Left: Original St. Peter's Catholic Church (date unknown). *A History of St. Peter's Church*, 1990. Courtesy of St. Peter's Catholic Church.

St. Peter's Catholic Cemetery. Photographed by the author.

References and Sources

Firsthand Accounts by Ursuline Convent Students and Columbia Residents

Crittenden, Mrs. S. A. "The Sack of Columbia." In *South Carolina Women in the Confederacy*, edited by Mrs. Thomas Taylor, Mrs. A. T. Smythe, Mrs. August Kohn, Miss M. B. Poppenheim, and Miss Martha B. Washington, State Committee Daughters of the Confederacy. Columbia, S.C.: The State Company, 1903. http://genealogytrails.com/scar/women_conf/woman_conf_10.htm.

Magrath, Selina Bollin. "Columbia Burning Horrors Recounted by Eye Witness." *Columbia Star,* February 13, 2015. Reprinted from the *Charleston News & Courier,* February 17, 1934.

Ravenel, Harriott H. "When Columbia Burned." In *South Carolina Women in the Confederacy*, edited by Mrs. Thomas Taylor, Mrs. A. T. Smythe, Mrs. August Kohn, Miss M. B. Poppenheim, and Miss Martha B. Washington, State Committee Daughters of the Confederacy. Columbia, S.C.: The State Company, 1903. http://genealogytrails.com/scar/women_conf/woman_conf_10.htm.

Richardson, Sara Aldrich. "The Burning of the Ursuline Convent by Sherman." In *South Carolina Women in the Confederacy*, edited by Mrs. Thomas Taylor, Mrs. A. T. Smythe, Mrs. August Kohn, Miss M. B. Poppenheim, and Miss Martha B. Washington, State Committee Daughters of the Confederacy. Columbia, S.C.: The State Company, 1903. http://genealogytrails.com/scar/women_conf/woman_conf_10.htm.

Books

Begni, Ernesto. "Ursuline Nuns: Independent Convents: Columbia, S.C.." In *The Catholic Church in the United States of America,* vol. 2, *The Religious Communities of Women,* 472–73. New York: Catholic Editing Company, 1914. https://books.google.com/books?id=x70YAAAAYAAJ&printsec=frontcover&source=gbs_ge_summary_r&cad=0#v=onepage&q&f=false.

Simms, William Gilmore. *Sack and Destruction of the City of Columbia, S.C.* Columbia, SC: Power Press of Daily Phœnix, 1865. http://simms.library.sc.edu/view_item.php?item=139109&tab=contents.

Newspaper Articles

"Interactive Map: Path of Sherman's troops through Columbia in February 1865." On-line special report of the *State,* January 17, 2015. http://www.thestate.com/news/special-reports/article13938536.html.

Wilkinson, Jeff, and contributors Joe Long, John Sherrer, and Tom Elmore. "Five Myths about the Burning of Columbia." Online special report of the *State,* February 13, 2015. http://www.thestate.com/news/local/article13953590.html.

Websites

Lt. Gen. Wade Hampton, Camp No. 273 Columbia, S.C., Sons of Confederate Veterans. "The Burning of Columbia." 1865 street map of Columbia, S.C. Accessed November 7, 2016. http://www.wadehamptoncamp.org/burn-cola1.jpg.

Public Broadcasting Service. "Civil War Facts." Accessed March 15, 2016. http://www.pbs.org/kenburns/civil-war/war/civil-war-facts/.

Sons of Confederate Veterans, Lt. Gen. Wade Hampton Camp No. 273. "Ursuline Mother Superior Sister Baptista Lynch Saves the Hampton House." Accessed June 16, 2014. http://www.wadehamptoncamp.org/hist-sb.html.